A COMPREHENSIVE GUIDE FOR CHOOSING AND INSTALLING RIGHT DOOR IN RIGHT WAY

JITENDRA K. GOYAL

Worldwide Published by
Pendown Press

PENDOWN PRESS LLP

An ISO 9001 & ISO 14001 Certified Co.,

Regd. Office: 3767A, Kanhaiya Nagar,
Tri Nagar, Delhi-110035

Ph.: 8130886000, 9650072927, 8595249536

E-mail: info@pendownpress.com

Branch Office: 1A/2A, 20, Hari Sadan, Ansari Road,
Daryaganj, New Delhi-110002

Ph.: 011-45794768

Website: PendownPress.com

First Edition: 2023

Price: ₹249/-

ISBN: 978-93-5554-619-7

Layout and Cover Designed by Pendown Graphics Team

Printed and Bound in India by Thomson Press India Ltd.

Unlock THE POTENTIAL of Your DOORS

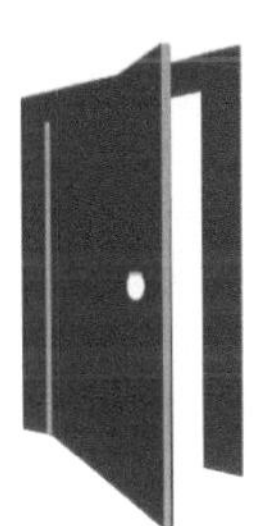

A COMPREHENSIVE GUIDE FOR CHOOSING AND INSTALLING RIGHT DOOR IN RIGHT WAY

*I dedicate this book to my father,
Sh. Kailash Chand Goyal, and mother,
Smt. Rama Devi Goyal, for their
unwavering trust, love, and support
throughout my journey.*

CONTENTS

FOREWORD

The author of this book has always fascinated me for his commitment to work. Whenever I think of him, the image that comes to mind is of a person willing to learn, passionate and hard-working, with an ability to think out of the box.

To be honest, for me 'Door and Difficulty' mean the same thing. I am not the kind of person who shall ever be able to understand 'how to choose a door' and how to understand the problems of buyers. All this makes my mind heavy.

But, when I encountered this book, I was impressed with the wealth of knowledge that he has related to doors. I have good reasons to believe that this book will provide suitable answers to all the questions that occupy the minds of the readers of this book and help them understand the intricacies of Doors and safeguard them from unnecessary difficulties and show them 'how engineered doors can enhance their experience multi-fold.

I am sure, this book will prove to be a treasure trove in the field of Doors and their selection.

~Pragat Dvivedi,

Founder Editor Ply Reporter

WHY THIS BOOK?

I have worked extensively in this industry and witnessed the struggles people face when purchasing doors. I am on a mission to ensure that everyone who needs a door can properly analyze their requirements and select the right product. Since I can't personally reach everyone,I decided to write this book to assist buyers in choosing and installing the right door that best suits their needs.

However, I wish that…

People start selecting the doors based on their functional value and the safety they provide,rather than solely for aesthetic reasons.

I want people to expect more from doors and considering them as catalysts for life safety and user experience.

With this book, I aim to shed light on the compromises people often make when it comes to choosing doors and jeopardizing safety.

ACKNOWLEDGEMENT

Our achievements are not solely the result of our own efforts; there is a multitude of people who help shape our lives and assist us in achieving milestones. I am blessed to have many individuals in my life who support me in various ways and inspire, support, and enable me on my journey.

I would like to acknowledge my entire family and elder members for creating an environment within the family where everyone can grow and choose their own path.

I extend my heartfelt thanks to Mr. Akshar Yadav for being a great mentor, pushing me to write this book, and standing by me throughout this journey.

I am grateful to Mr. Dinesh Verma, CEO of Pendown Publication House, and his team for their support and suggestions throughout the creative process. As an entrepreneur, you can only pursue your personal passion if you have a team that can take care of your business.

I am thankful to the entire team at Dormak, including Mr. Mayank, Mr. Vijay, Ms. Sapna, Mr. Pradeep, Mr. Sunil, Mr. Dinesh, Mr. Pankaj, and Ms. Meenakshi. They are true leaders in their fields, and their insights have helped me better understand the market.

Special thanks to my wife, Suman, who holds me accountable and keeps me moving forward.

Much love to my daughter, Navika, and my son, Iksheet. They are my energy boosters.

Chapter 1

INTRODUCTION

I am a door expert, with 15 years of experience in the door industry. I have successfully delivered over 2 million doors. I have conducted extensive research on the door market and consistently prioritize the functionality of doors. Simultaneously, I am dedicated to developing and delivering doors that are operationally stable and create a positive user experience.

All my efforts are aimed at making the industry more efficient, saving time, and ensuring quick installations of specialized doors designed for specific requirements. Our goal is to provide a hassle-free experience with international quality.

I am grateful to my team, our esteemed dealers, and customers for helping me establish a strong reputation in the door industry and referring to me with confidence.

At Dormak, we constantly innovate our products and strive for a greener tomorrow. We are committed to deliver state-of-art, high-quality doors to our customers.

Hello, my name is Jitendra Goyal, I am the founder and managing director of Dormak Interio Pvt. Ltd. We are a 15 year experienced company specializing in doors and turnkey door projects. With the widest range of doors available, and we have successfully delivered 2 million doors.

In the year 2005, I was involved in the business of retailing interior products when I realized that there was a lack of and limited knowledge and limited options in the field of doors. The choices were mainly limited to wooden panel doors or flush doors, which followed a one-size-fits-all approach. Regardless of specific requirements, people would simply take a flush door and attempt to adapt it for various uses. This led to relying on 6-7 different vendors for (Raw materials), without a single vendor taking accountability for problem-solving.

Recognizing this gap in the market, I decided to delve deeper into the subject and enhance my knowledge. I began studying international trends in the door market exploring the various solutions available to cater to specific requirements. I sought to understand the science behind the doors and their functionality.

After conducting extensive research and making international visits, I finally established Dormak in 2008 with the sole objective of providing specialized doors as per norms and cater to specific applications. We conducted thorough research on various door cores and their applications to optimize the performance of our doors.

We began with a smaller unit covering an area of 1700 square meters, and today we have expanded 20,000 square meter unit. Throughout our journey, we have served over 2 million doors, gaining the trust of more than 3000 satisfied customers. Additionally, we successfully fulfilled a single export order worth over $1 million. We have had the privilege of working with India's most prestigious projects and hospitality industry.

The current scenario in the industry is to get a reliable specific product with assurance and promise to deliver on time.

And our product offerings are designed to address these needs, with international affiliations and standardization that allow us to deliver large quantities on time. Our optimized installation process ensures timely delivery, ultimately increasing the return on investment (ROI) for our customers.

Our promise is to revolutionize the door industry and provide life safety to people by offering proper doors that serve in fire and sound, while also saving the mother earth by using environmentally friendly products.

I am on a mission of safety and optimizing the functionality of doors through awareness and proper installation.

So let's delve deep into it. My challenge is that there is so much unexplored potential in doors that can save lives and provide quality sleep and work environments, ultimately saving millions of dollars by choosing the right product.

Imagine what will happen when we start trusting experts and selecting the right product for specific needs. This will conserve our energy and allow us to focus on truly matters, all while improving our overall quality of life.

Let's build a world together that prioritizes specificity, optimization, and user experience.

Chapter 2

PROBLEMS OF CUSTOMERS

There are lots of problems and challenges to the door market in India. Here, I will address some of the most common issues:

1. **Lack of Information and Expertise:**

   Many buyers may lack adequate information and expertise when it comes to selecting wooden doors. They may be unaware of the various types of doors available, their specific characteristics, and how to assess the quality of a door. This lack of knowledge can make the selection process overwhelming and increase the risk of making an uninformed decision. To provide further elaboration, I will categorize this problem into sub-points.

   A. Staging of the door - At what stage one should take decision on doors and frames and usually house owners buy the frame at primary construction stage without keeping in mind the door and functionality and end up compromising on safety and door quality.

   B. Not considering the door as a whole - Often, the door frame, door shutter and hardware are seen as different part of the door and never work it out as a whole. The performance of these components is optimized when they are planned and intalled together.

C. Not knowing the option in the market- Customer are often unaware of the latest trends and advancements in the door market, as well as the wide range of door products available.

2. Lack of Standardization:

In India, the lack of standardization in the sizing and dimensions of wooden doors is a common issue. This poses challenges when it comes to replacing existing doors or maintaining a consistent look throughout a property. Buyers may struggle to find doors that perfectly fit their door frames, resulting in increased inventories for dealers. Moreover, the production process at manufacturing facilities can be negatively affected as they struggle to meet the demand for doors of specific sizes.

3. Lack of adaptability:

There is a myth in the market and that runs the market.

This myth revolves around people's attachment to traditional wooden doors and feeling that doors should only be made of wood and they accompanied by limited knowledge and adaptability to new age engineered wooden products, which are better in terms of life, operational functionality, life, finish and ease of use.

4. Unwillingness of dealers and service providers.

In the door market, approximately 85% of the decision-making process is influenced by dealers and contractors. However, there is a common issue where dealers are not willing to understand the buyer's specific requirements and provide proper consultancy. Instead, they prioritize selling the products they have in stock or what they want. Similarly, contractors tend to stick to their comfort zone and resist adopting ready-made door sets or specialize doors. This lack of willingness from dealers and contractors hinders the buyer's ability to make informed choices and find the most suitable door solutions.

Chapter 3

HOW TO CHOOSE A DOOR

"You Are free to choose, but you are not free from the consequence of your choice."

Here, I would like to discuss the factors that needs to be considered, and later on, we will discuss upon the common myths in the door industry.

Additionally, I want to share the story of my friend, Rajesh Sharma, and his experiences.

When he found out that I specialize in custom-made doors and consultancy in selection of doors, he shared his own experience with me. During the construction of his house, he was advised by many to install stone frames, so he followed that recommendation. However, when it came the time to install the actual doors, he contacted a contractor who provided him with a design book for doors. Unfortunately, the door design he chose couldn't be made in a lower thickness, and the stone supplier had already made a rebate of 30mm, which couldn't be altered at that point..

Consequently, he had to settle for a laminated door that could be supplied in a 30mm thickness. The contractor purchased the door, but it did not come in the exact sizes required, so they had to cut and modify the door on-site to make it fit. As a result, Rajesh is now facing a lot of issues. Firstly, he can't achieve the premium appearance he desired with a 30mm thick door, And the stone frames are not complimenting his interior.

Additionally, the doors, like many others that have been cut on-site, are experiencing loosening of screws, and the laminates are cracking due to a lack of knowledge about the quality and proper pasting procedures.

Here is an another example:

I have visited the house of our acquaintance, Mr. Sanjeev Jain. They have installed beautifully crafted doors with a white PU finish. However, when I saw the frame, I noticed yellow stains on it. Upon closer analysis, I discovered that they used a good quality teak wood frame, and the wood was releasing yellow pigmentation from within, which appeared on top of the PU paint.

Therefore, when selecting a frame, one should consider the desired final finish carefully.

Hence, it is crucial to consult about doors from the planning stage itself. Once the frame is installed, nearly 50% of door options may no longer be feasible or available on-site and we have to plan everything as per that frame.

Selection of door depends upon various factors and we are discussing few of the major key factors:

1. **Where to use it (Type of project):**

   A door installed in a residential apartment may appear similar to one in a hospitality project, and doors in hostels and hospitals may also seem alike at first glance.. However, it's important to note that there are significant differences in terms of door structure and functionality. These variances primarily arise from the specific requirements of each project and the utilization of different hardware. What is the end result we want to achieve?

2. **Location of the door in project:**

   Where it is placed in your house also plays an important role. Here we are taking the example of a residence.

   A Main door construction is different from the internal door, with safety being the primary requirement for the former, while privacy takes precedence for internal bedroom or bathroom doors.

   A bedroom door can be simple in design and made with different core materials compared to the main door.

   A Bathroom door- depends upon the size of the bathroom and the presence of wet area in the bathroom. The structure and finish of the door are also important factors, especially if the door is in direct contact with showers or water. Additionally, the choice of bathroom door depends on whether the bathroom is used in a dry or wet manner.

A Kitchen door- In the case of a kitchen door, options such as a glass panel or a fire-rated door are available. And it has been seen people using sliding doors in the kitchen.

A Balcony door- this do structure, design, and finish to prevent bending and to maintain the finish over an extended period..

A Living room door- This door is designed as per the interior of the lobby or any glass panel is required.

A Pooja room door- This door is designed as per culture and religious factors, as well as the need for appropriate lighting inside the sacred space.

3. **Purpose of the door:**

As we discussed the location of the door, and at each location the purpose of the door is different, mainly we deal with the purposes of safety, security, light, and design. However, in addition to these purposes, we must also consider fire safety, acoustics (noise reduction), kids safety, zero toxicity. These aspects need to be taken into careful consideration.

Functionality of the door: Need to consider the functionality of the door in terms of whether it opens as a single or double, and whether it is a sliding or swing door. Also need to see the space around the door and choose the appropriate type accordingly. For instance, bi-fold doors and four-fold doors are commonly used in terrace and balcony areas.

4. **Structure of the project:**

   Structure plays an important role in selection of doors, choosing a main door for a villa is different from selecting a main door for a building. The doors in a hotel will vary from those in an open resort. The main door of a single or double-story building is different from the main door of a flat on the 20th floor.

   On the 20th floor, it is necessary to provide a higher fire rating, considering the escape time. Therefore, based on the structure of the project, we need to carefully choose the door type, design, and specifications of the doors.

5. **Design and Aesthetic element:**

   The design and finish are visible aspects that require careful attention to achieve perfection and optimization. Depending on the top surface and design, we need to choose the appropriate door and determine its thickness.

   Door works on the principle of balancing. Both sides of the door should receive the same treatment and be made of the same material to make it workable. However, in certain cases, different finishes and designs are required on each side due to design considerations. In such cases, a special treatment and core selection are necessary to maintain the door's straightness.

   At many places, the door needs to be flushed with the front wall and concealed. In these situations, a specialized door and its design are selected to achieve the desired outcome.

6. **Height of the door:**

   One door cannot fulfill all requirements. However, it is believed that a flush door available in the market can be fitted in heights ranging from 7 feet to 12 feet.

   Making a door above 8 feet requires a completely different approach, including considerations for the rails, stiles, and inner core of the door.

7. **Hardware selection (type of hardware):**

   Doors and hardware are designed to complement each other. Neither can perform effectively alone. There is an evolution in the hardware industry that enhances the workability and aesthetics of doors. To fit it right, we need to choose the right door. To ensure a proper fit, it is essential to choose the right door while also considering the availability of compatible hardware. There are certain types of hinges, door closers, and locks that requires specific thickness and provisions in the door to get the desired results.

   While we invest lots of money in quality hardware, it is crucial to also consider the installation capabilities of the professionals who will be fixing the doors. Do they have the right tools, fixtures, and skills to do it? Failure to install the hardware properly can turn a seemingly convenient feature into a nightmare.

8. Building code and Norms.

There exist building codes and advisory guidelines for uses of doors as per project. The Bureau of Indian Standards (BIS) provides codes and specifications for doors to be used in various contexts such as the military (ARMY), railways, airports, and high-rise apartments. It is crucial to adhere to these codes and specifications when selecting doors for such applications.

Budget:

Budget is an important aspect, and different types of residential apartments or houses have different budget considerations. Based on the available budget, we can make decisions regarding the core, finish, design, and thickness of the door.

While budget is a significant factor, it is possible to select a good door without compromising on quality that offers functional stability and value. Budget should be clearly discussed with the consultant or professional so that they can provide suitable product options. Often, people hide their budget and start looking for cheaper products and compromise on quality By sharing the budget upfront, there is no need to compromise on quality, and better recommendations can be provided.

9. Green rating:

There is a growing consciousness towards green building and environmental friendly products. Some projects require a green building certification or LEED rating. In such cases, it is important to use doors that have obtained a green certification. Additionally, various projects may require doors that are certified by the Forest Stewardship Council (FSC) or the Programme for the Endorsement of Forest Certification (PEFC). Many individual house owners also prefer to use VOC (Volatile Organic Compound) free doors. That helps in circulating green air in the door and these doors are free from any toxic compound and chemical.

And this can be done irrespective of any design and specifications.

10. Atmosphere (climate):

A door in Kashmir is different from a door in Goa. Extensive research has been conducted in the door industry, and when it comes to internal doors, they can remain the same in different climatic conditions as long as they are properly sealed and protected against the climate, but for external doors, we need to carefully choose the finish and design as per specific climate requirements.

11. User experience of the door:

User experience is something that has always existed but often went unidentified and overlooked. Different types of hardware and finishes provide various types of user experience in terms of touch and feel. In terms of soft opening and closing mechanisms and impact the overall design and appearance of the door on the wall. Therefore, the door is designed with the ultimate user experience in mind, aiming to achieve specific desired outcomes.

12. Door Jamb (Frame):

I always recommend that the door should be bought with a door jamb (door frame) as a complete assembly. Doors perform better when both components are planned and installed together by professionals.

In many cases, frames are installed at an earlier stage. When selecting a door, it is important to consider the type and rebate of the frame. For stone, cement and metal frames, no amendments can be made, and the thickness of the door should be as per the door jamb rebate. Hardware selection should also be as per the type of frame.

13. How fast things need to get done:

There is a time schedule and sequence of tasks in each project. When the things gets faster then the material and finish of the door should be chosen in such a way that the faster delivery can be made and flawless doors can be installed within that time.

Chapter 4

HOW TO SAFEGUARD THE DOOR FROM EXPANSION AND CONTRACTION?

To safeguard a wooden door from expansion and contraction, you can take several measures:

i. **Proper Installation:**

Ensure that the door is installed correctly according to the manufacturer's guidelines. This includes ensuring that there is adequate clearance around the door frame to accommodate natural expansion and contraction. (We recommend a 3 mm air gap on the left, right and top of the door, and 5-6 mm gap at the bottom). Improper installation can lead to unnecessary stress on the door, resulting in warping or bending.

ii. **Seal and Finish:**

Apply a finishing material to the surfaces of the door that stops or prevents the moisture absorption, such as laminates or PVC surfaces. In the case of veneers and wood, apply a high-quality sealer and top coat to both the exterior and interior surfaces. A sealer or finish helps to protect the wood from moisture absorption, which is a leading cause of expansion and contraction. Ensure that all side edges of the doors are properly sealed with beading, edge band, or a thick application of sealant paint.

It forms a barrier that reduces the impact of environmental changes on the dimensions of the door.

iii. Humidity Control:

Maintain proper humidity levels in the surrounding environment. Wood tends to expand in high humidity and contract in low humidity.

iv. Ventilation:

Ensure that the area where the door is located is properly ventilated. Good airflow can help regulate the humidity levels and prevent moisture buildup, which can contribute to excessive expansion or contraction of the wooden door.

v. Avoid direct sunlight and heat sources:

Protect the wooden door from direct sunlight and heat sources. Prolonged exposure to intense sunlight of proximity to a fireplace can cause the wood to dry out and shrink, leading to potential warping or cracking. We can use blinds and curtains to reduce sunlight exposure and maintain a more stable temperature around the door.

vi. **Repair of cracks and damages:**

Perform regular inspection or maintenance of the door and repair any damage or cracks in the door or frame.

By implementing these measures, you can minimize the effects of expansion and contraction on your wooden door. Remember that wood is a natural material and will naturally experience some degree of movement over time. However, proper installation, sealing, humidity control, and maintenance can help mitigate these issues and prolong the lifespan of wooden doors.

Chapter 5

COMMON MYTH AND QUESTIONS ABOUT THE DOOR

(A) Door should be wooden, or in the case of a flush door, it should be wood filled.

As we have grown since our childhood we have seen the association of wood with doors and windows. So we have started asking for wood filler even in the flush door. Here we need to understand the role of filler in the door, and what it does in the door. And what are the alternative options of the wood filler and how that helps the door in performing in a better way.

Why did we start using wood as a filler?

The time when we started making the flush door, all the components were made out of wood, which was abundantly available. Additionally, the same manufacturers who produced the doors also had access to wood, making it a convenient and compatible material for the manufacturing process. During that time, alternatives (engineered material) for filling were not available. Wood filling is a good process and performed well over a long period of time. However, it does have certain limitations, that's why other materials were invented.

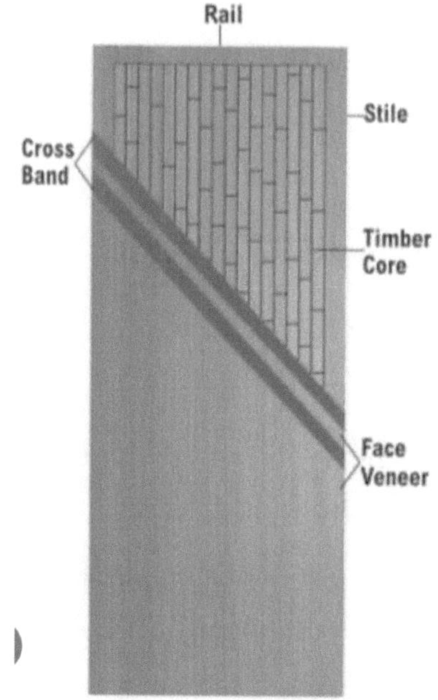

Limitations of wood filler

1. It is a labor-intensive work.
2. Difficult to manage the same standard of filling all time.
3. It is difficult to get standard wood available at all times.
4. It increases the weight of the door.
5. It can be costly and unnecessary in certain cases.
6. Producers may find it easier to manipulate and use mixed and substandard wood.
7. It has a waviness on the surface.
8. Certain types of finishes, such as high gloss and PU paint, cannot be performed on wood-filled doors.

Alternative filler option and its advantages

Particle Board Core (Filler): This particle board is manufactured in various thickness using chips of different woods, primarily pinewood chips with a density ranging from 425kg to 475kg/CBM. It is produced using a flat press machine. It is a subtle material and can be evenly filled into the door.

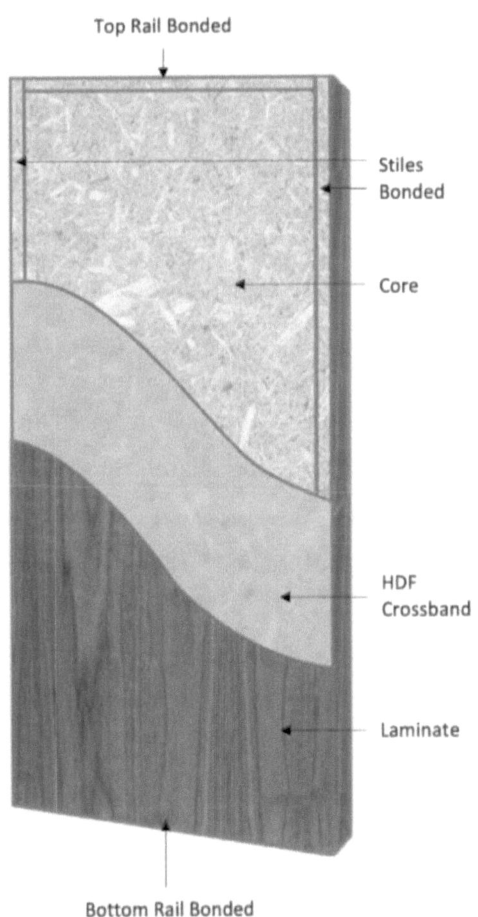

Advantage of particle board

1. It offers consistent thickness, eliminating undulation on the door surface.
2. It has excellent screw holding capacity, allowing for secure fittings of various types.
3. Due to its calibrated and even thickness, particle board enables achieving finishes such as high gloss and PU paint on the door.
4. It is cost-effective.
5. It saves the time of filling, resulting in higher productivity.
6. It offers material consistency, ensuring the same quality and finish at all times.

Tubular Particle board

It is an advanced material. that was invented in Germany by a company called Sauerland Spanplatte. They have done intense research in developing this product. It is available in various thickness and is manufactured using a specialized extrusion technique.

Advantage of tubular particle board

1. It provides fire resistance, enhancing the door's fire rating.
2. It provides acoustical properties.
3. It exhibits high stability. There are less chances of bending or wrapping in the door.
4. There is no telegraphy and waviness on the surface of the door.
5. It reduces the weight of the door.

6. It is a specialized material with green certification, promoting environmentally friendly practices.
7. Particle board, with its advanced technology, supports the construction of taller doors, such as 9 feet or 10 feet, providing stability and even load distribution in these larger doors.

Honeycomb Core

It has been developed for a specialized market catering to specialized doors. It offers several advantages over other cores. However, it is important to note that its applications are limited.

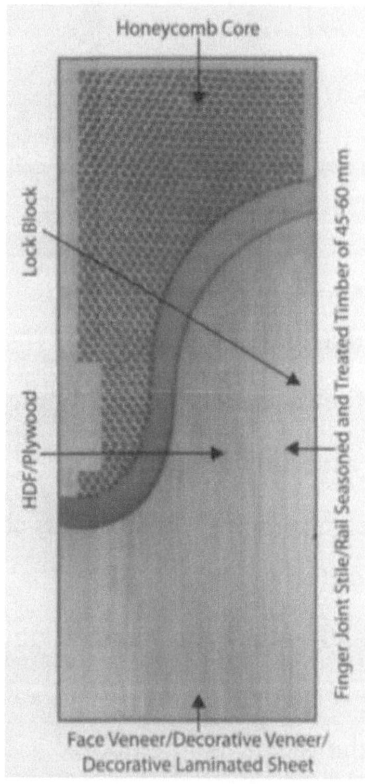

Advantage of Honeycomb Core

1. It is light in weight
2. It is cost-effective.
3. It does not utilize wood in its construction, resulting in conservation of wood resources.
4. Assembling and manufacturing doors with honeycomb core is relatively easier compared to other core materials.

Disadvantages

1. Not all types of doors can be made using this core material.
2. Honeycomb core is typically used in doors that require specific functionalities or cost effectiveness.

What do I suggest

I always suggest going with a particle board core, whether it's solid wood particle or tubular particle. Both options are good, But for specialized products and better results, I highly recommend using tubular particle board core as it provides additional features.

(B) Why should we use a higher thickness door?

There is a myth in the market questioning the need for higher thickness doors. Some argue that doors of 30mm and 25mm can serve the purpose just as well, while others believe that increasing the door thickness will significantly raise the cost.However, it is important to understand the advantages of opting for higher thickness doors and the issues associated with lower thickness doors.

Looking at the global scenario, countries across Europe, U.S and UAE adhere to a standard door thickness of 44mm.

There are various advantages of Thicker door:

1. They can accommodate various types of hardware, including digital locks and door closers.
2. When we increase the thickness of the door, it looks more stable and gives a sturdy feeling.
3. Thicker doors have reduced chances of bending or warping, and they can achieve higher acoustical ratings and even a 30-minute fire rating.
4. They allow for more design options, such as paneling and grooving.
5. It gives a pure value addition, the door of 44mm looks rich and all kinds of hardware can be fixed very well so it's a better preposition.
6. There is a prevailing myth and misconception that increasing the thickness of a door directly corresponds to a significant increase in price. However, this is not the case. In reality, when we opt for a thicker door, the price does not increase proportionally. The incremental cost is relatively minimal compared to the added value and benefits we gain from the thicker door.

(C) Can I trust the quality of factory finished doors?

It has always been considered that things getting done in front of our eyes provide better results and give longevity and we can rely upon the material used.

This perception emerged during a time when testing facilities were scarce and manual craftsmanship prevailed. However, as we now prioritize efficiency, quality, and impeccable finishes, the demand for factory-finished products has surged. So, what are the advantages of factory finishing and why should we go for it?

1. **Advance technique of manufacturing:** At the manufacturing plant, state-of-the-art machinery and advanced technologies are utilized to precise and standardized production processes. Comprehensive training is provided by machinery and raw material manufacturers to get the best output. Additionally, factories are equipped with laboratories to maintain consistent quality control measures. Even the adhesive which is typically done manually on-site, can be efficiently spread using glue spreaders or applicators. This method ensures optimal adhesive distribution and yields superior results that would be challenging to achieve otherwise.
2. **Technical knowhow and certification:** The personnel working at the plant are equipped with required know how about the uses of various raw materials and its application. Furthermore, the final product and the manufacturing processes undergo certification to ensure the consistent delivery of high-quality products every time.

3. **Standard raw material and testing of the door:** When it comes to making the door in the plant, then all sourced raw materials are accompanied by standard technical data sheets and specifications. A proper application training is given. Moreover, there is a systematic checking system implemented at various stages of the door production to ensure optimal efficiency and quality.
4. **Fixing of hardware and optimize uses of it:** Hardware has evolved to become an integral part of the doors with a wide range of premium and specialized options available. Installing such hardware requires specific machine tools and the use of a CNC machine, which can only be operated using dedicated software and proper training. This is the function which optimize the functionality of doors and provides long-lasting results and that can only be achieved with professional installation.

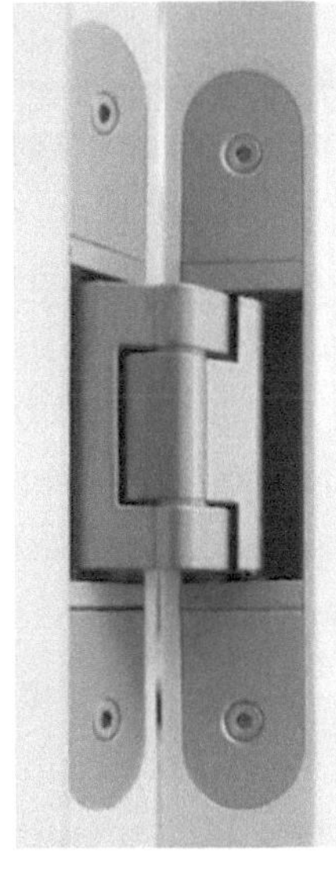

5. **Superior finish:** The door manufactured in plants offer a superior finish due to the coating process carried out on specialized UV and PU lines, with proper curing techniques. At the plant, the ratio and application of coatings can be checked, and testing equipment is readily available. This attention to minute details contributes to the achievement of a superior finish for the doors.
6. **Fast implementation:** With the utilization of high-capacity advanced equipment and machinery, projects can be delivered at a faster pace in the plant. The doors are manufactured according to the design specifications set by professionals, eliminating the need for revisiting and inspecting at various stages. In contrast, work done on-site requires inspection and cannot guarantee the same level of time commitment.

7. **Costing of the door:** When purchasing raw materials individually, it becomes challenging to accurately calculate the exact cost of the door. Relying on multiple vendors for various components such as the basic door, laminate, veneer, adhesive, painter, and carpenter often leads to discrepancies and wastage. On the other hand, when working with a factory, the provided costing becomes the final product cost, ensuring transparency and accuracy.

   Many people calculate the cost, but often overlook additional expenses such as supervision costs, wastage, and hidden painting costs. These costs only visible once the painter presents the bill, as their measurements can increase overall expenses.

8. **Overall Guarantee:** When purchasing a factory-finished door, the buyer deals with a single vendor who handles the entire process from door manufacturing to installation. On the other hand, with doors made on-site, there can be up to eight different vendors involved in the process, leading to a lack of accountability. In case of any issues or problems, each vendor tends to shift blame onto others, such as the flush door, adhesive, laminate, veneer, or even the carpenter responsible for improper application. This lack of responsibility makes it challenging to obtain a proper resolution for the problem at hand.

Here is a Case Study

It is about my friend Manish, a premium builder from Jaipur known for constructing high-end residences. He invited me to visit one of his newly built apartments. Upon arrival, I noticed several people working in one of the flats. Curious, I asked Manish about their purpose, and he explained that they were cleaning the floors, removing polish marks from the walls, and performing various cleaning tasks. I pointed out that the work seemed complete, so why was it being redone? Manish replied, "A customer is visiting tomorrow, and I want to ensure the flat is perfectly finished."

This additional work incurs unwanted costs and often fails to deliver a flawless output and finish. To address this issue, the solution lies in opting for factory-finished products. By utilizing such products, builders can achieve a perfect finish, eliminating the need for last-minute touch-ups and ensuring customer satisfaction.

By implementing factory finishes, builders like Manish can save time, costs, and effort associated with post-construction work. This approach guarantees a flawless outcome, impressing customers with the quality of work delivered.

(D) Should we match the door to the interior?

While selecting a door, I see people always give emphasis to their interior like this particular color, this particular design is not matching to our Interior. We want to match it with our interior.

In some parts of India, I have seen people doing wall to wall interiors where the door becomes an integral part of the interior design. In these cases, different designs are applied to the front and back sides of the door, aligning with the specific interior style of each room.

So there is a practice of matching the interior with the door at some places.

Particularly in the hotel industry.

While there is no harm in doing so, it is worth noting that conceptually, doors and interiors in the residential sector are typically not perfectly matched. Globally, doors and windows are considered separate elements from the interior, and the work of installing them is often handled by different agencies.

We should design a door in such a way that it complements the interior and it becomes an integral part of that interior. It should neither be too different nor identical to the interior, but rather harmonize with it. In the past, doors were typically made before interior work was done, using materials such as wood or other materials.

Doors, windows and furniture all are considered joinery work and are often handled by different vendors in residential projects. By planning wisely and involving professionals, we can save time during the execution and ensure a cohesive and well-integrated result.

(E) Which way of door frame installation should be adopted?

There are two ways of installing a door frame:

1. **Wet way of fixing-** In this method, we purchase the wood months before installation. The wood is then dried and fixed in place before the flooring and plastering process. Hold fasteners are used to secure the frame to the brick wall, with the bottom of the frame positioned below the floor level.

   The frame is installed in its raw condition, and the finishing is done later on.

   Advantage

   i. Frames get a very strong bonding by cement and mortar. However, the actual strength required for the frame is a matter of consideration.

   Disadvantage

   ii. Cracks develop in frames due to curing.

   iii. Color and shade of doors and frame is difficult to match.

- **iv.** Various type of acoustical and fire rating cannot be achieved.
- **v.** Proper installation of various types of hardware becomes problematic.
- **vi.** There is lack of accuracy the width of the door is not consistent at all levels.

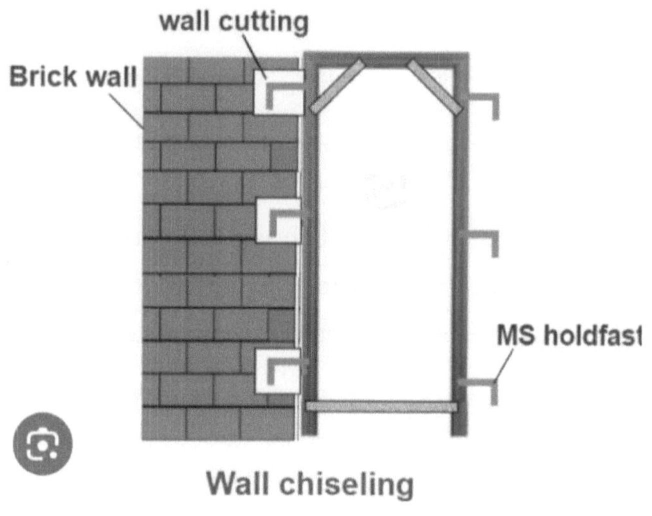

2. **Dry way of fixing-** In dry way of fixing, the frame is installed after the floor, plaster, and curing processes. I recommend installing it even after applying POP and the first coat of paint.

   The Frame is fixed using PU Foam and Fasteners, and there are various ways to install it and hide the fastener from the door frame.

Advantage

i. A matching door and frame can be installed, providing a perfect finish.

ii. Saves time at the site as it is done during the final finishing stage.

iii. It saves the door and frame from termites, as the frame is installed away from the wall and with the help of foam.

iv. As it is done by professionals so all type of functional hardware can be installed optimally.

v. Frame material is properly seasoned in this method, ensuring it remains crack free and finish remains intact.

vi. The fixing method of PU Foam and specialised fastners provide high stability and superior holding, this can sustain even very high wind velocity in high raise building.

Chapter 6

FIRE RATED DOORS

Why should I use a fire-rated wooden door?

Fire-rated wooden doors offer several important advantages when it comes to safety and protection in buildings and houses. Here are some reasons why you should consider using fire-rated wooden doors.

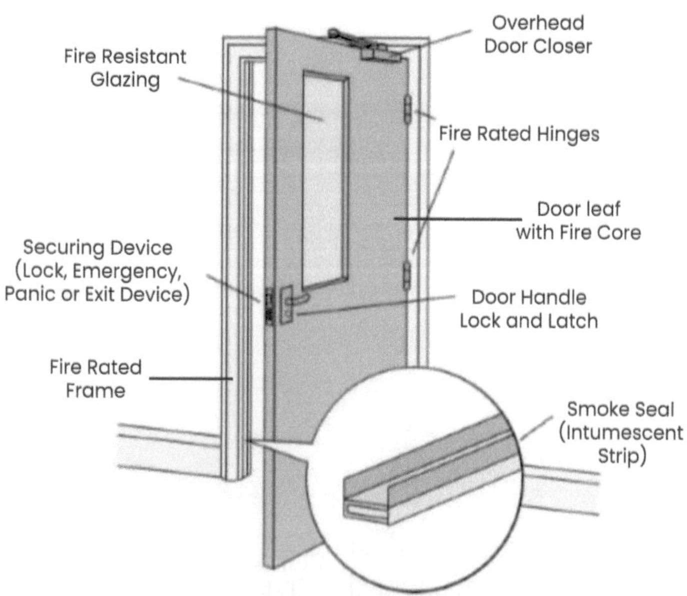

Fire Rated Door

Fire Protection

Fire-rated wooden doors are specifically designed to resist the spread of fire and smoke. These doors are specifically designed with fire-resistant materials and are tested to withstand fire for a specified period, typically ranging from 30 minutes to 120 minutes. These doors act as a barrier, limiting the fire's ability to spread and providing valuable time for occupants to evacuate the building.

Code Compliance

In many cases, building codes and regulations mandate the installation of fire-rated doors in specific areas of a building, including fire exits, stairwells, corridors, and rooms housing flammable materials. Additionally, fire-rated wooden doors are commonly used as the main doors for flats, hotel rooms, and master bedrooms. By opting for fire-rated wooden doors, you guarantee compliance with these essential safety regulations.

Property Protection

Fire-rated wooden doors not only safeguard lives but also play a crucial role in minimizing property damage during a fire incident. By slowing down the fire's progression, these doors effectively contain it within a specific area, preventing its spread to other parts of the building. This containment significantly reduces overall damage and facilitates smoother firefighting operations.

Aesthetics and Design Flexibility

Wooden doors are highly regarded for their natural and elegant aesthetic appeal, making them a popular choice in many buildings. Fire-rated wooden doors bring together in fire protection and visual appeal, offering a diverse selection of designs to suit various architectural styles and interior preferences. This allows you to maintain a consistent design theme throughout the building without compromising on safety.

Durability and Performance

Fire-rated wooden doors are engineered to withstand the harsh conditions of a fire. They undergo rigorous testing procedures to ensure their resistance to fire, smoke, heat, insulation and structural integrity. Additionally, these doors are designed for durability, offering reliable performance over an extended period of time.

Sound Insulation

Fire-rated wooden doors can also provide sound insulation properties, making them advantageous in buildings where noise control is crucial, such as offices, hotels, or educational institutions. They effectively reduce the transfer of sound between different areas, contributing to a quieter and more comfortable environment.

When considering fire-rated wooden doors, it is essential to ensure that they are properly certified and installed by professionals. Always consult local building codes and regulations to determine the specific requirements (for commercial, residential and private houses) for your building to ensure the highest level of safety and compliance.

How does fire rated door works

Fire-rated wooden doors are specifically designed and constructed to resist fire and limit its spread. They achieve this through a combination of fire-resistant materials, construction techniques, and specialized components. Here's a general overview of how fire-rated wooden doors work:

Fire-Resistant Materials

Fire-rated wooden doors are made using materials that have undergone testing and certification for their fire resistance. The core of the door is typically composed of fire-rated timber, composite materials, or materials such as calcium silicate or magnesium oxide, which can withstand high temperatures. These materials are carefully chosen for their ability to resist fire, heat, and smoke. Both the door leaf and door jamb are designed to resist the fire.

Fire-rated wooden doors are assigned a specific fire rating, which indicates the amount of time they can withstand fire while maintaining their structural integrity and insulation. Common fire ratings include 30 minutes, 60 minutes, and 120 minutes. The fire rating of a door is determined by its construction and the materials used in its manufacturing process.

Intumescent Seals

Fire-rated wooden doors are equipped with intumescent seals. These seals are typically located around the edges of the door and in the door frame. In the event of a fire, the intumescent seals expand when exposed to heat, creating a barrier that restricts the passage of smoke and flames. This crucial feature helps to compartmentalize the fire and prevent its rapid spread.

Fire-Resistant Glazing

Some fire-rated wooden doors may incorporate fire-resistant glazing or vision panels. These glazing materials are specifically designed to endure high temperatures and prevent the spread of fire and smoke, all while maintaining visibility. Fire-rated glazing may include special glass, ceramic glass, or laminated glass with fire-resistant interlayers.

Fire Hardware

Fire hardware and its mechanism play a vital role in meeting the required fire rating and complying with safety normsThis hardware includes hinges, mortise locks, door closers and panic bar.

Fire-rated wooden doors are typically equipped with self-closing mechanisms, such as overhead door closers or concealed closers. These mechanisms ensure that the door automatically closes and securely latches in the event of a fire, helping to maintain the integrity of the fire barrier and prevents the passage of smoke and flames.

Compliance with Standards

Fire-rated wooden doors must adhere to specific standards and undergo rigorous testing to ensure their fire resistance and performance. Standards such as the National building code or local building codes outline the requirements for fire-rated doors, including their construction, fire ratings, hardware, and installation.

During a fire, a fire-rated wooden door acts as a barrier, effectively resisting the spread of fire and smoke between different areas of a building. By compartmentalizing the fire, these doors provide occupants with protected escape routes and offer firefighters the necessary time to control the fire and carry out rescue operations.

It's important to note that the effectiveness of fire-rated wooden doors relies on proper installation, regular maintenance, and adherence to fire safety protocols. Routine inspections and testing are necessary to ensure that the doors remain in good working condition and maintain their fire resistance capabilities over time.

A Case Study on Selecting Doors with Safety Considerations

There was a fire in a premium bungalow in Jaipur, and the house owner and kids died. The bungalow was beautifully designed with exclusive interior work. After conducting research, the firemen concluded that the cause of death for all victims was smoke inhalation. Since the fire occurred at midnight, they were unable to escape, and the smoke entered the room.

The question that arises is: could these lives have been saved by using the right door? Yes, if the consultant had suggested and installed fire doors in the bedrooms and kitchen, the smoke would not have entered the room from a specific direction, thereby potentially saving the occupants' lives. Fire doors are designed to prevent smoke from entering a room.

Chapter 7

ACOUSTIC DOORS

Acoustical doors (Sound proof) and how it works?

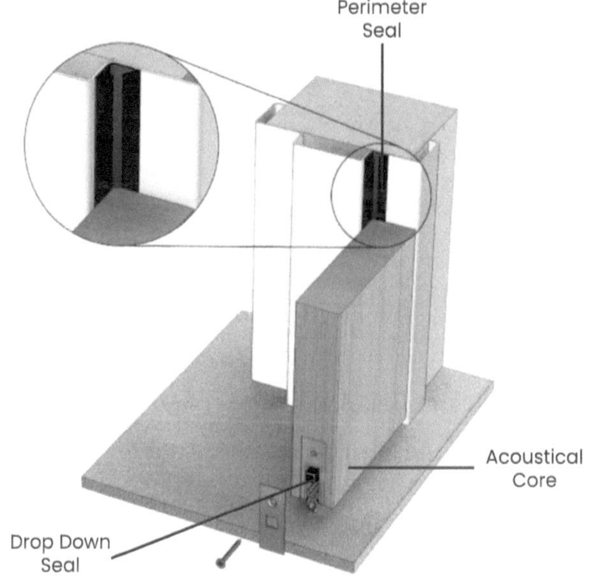

Acoustic Door

A wooden acoustical door, also reffered to as a soundproof or acoustic door, is specifically designed to minimize the transmission of sound between spaces. These doors are constructed using specific materials and techniques that aid in absorbing, blocking, or dampening sound waves, thereby reducing noise transfer. Here's an overview of how wooden acoustical doors work.

Construction and Materials

Wooden acoustical doors are typically constructed with multiple layers of wood or wood-based materials, such as particle board or medium-density fiberboard (MDF). These layers may be arranged in a staggered manner or filled with sound-absorbing materials like mineral wool, cork sheet or acoustic foam to enhance sound insulation. The door's construction helps to prevent sound waves from easily passing through it.

Mass and Density

The mass and density of the door play a crucial role in its soundproofing capabilities. The incorporation of multiple layers and dense materials in the construction of the door aids in blocking sound transmission. Thicker and heavier doors generally offer superior sound insulation compared to thinner and lighter doors.

Sealing Mechanisms

Acoustical doors are designed with tight seals around their edges to minimize sound leakage. These seals, typically made of materials like neoprene or rubber gaskets, ensure a proper fit between the door and the door frame. The seals help to prevent sound waves from escaping through gaps or cracks, thereby improving the overall soundproofing performance.

Sound Isolation Features

Wooden acoustical doors can include additional sound isolation features, including perimeter seals, threshold seals, and drop-down seals. These features further enhance the door's capability to prevent sound leakage and improve the overall soundproofing performance.

Hardware and Latching Systems

Acoustical doors are commonly equipped with specialized hardware and latching systems designed to maintain a tight and secure closure. This ensure that the door remains properly sealed, and minimizes sound transmission effectively.

Testing and Ratings

Acoustical doors undergo testing and receive ratings based on their sound transmission class (STC) performance. These ratings indicate the door's effectiveness in reducing sound transmission within specific frequency ranges. Higher STC ratings represent superior soundproofing performance.

Wooden acoustical doors are commonly used in environments where noise control is of utmost important, such as recording studios, theaters, conference rooms, music practice rooms, or any space that requires privacy and noise reduction. They provide a barrier against sound waves, helping to create a quieter and more controlled environment.

It's important to note that the effectiveness of a wooden acoustical door relies not only on the door itself but also on its proper installation, including the door frame, seals, and the overall construction of the surrounding walls. Consulting with acoustic professionals or manufacturers specializing in soundproofing can assist in determining the specific requirements and options to achieve optimal sound insulation in a given space.

Chapter 8

MY RECOMMENDATIONS

I urge every door user to carefully choose their doors, taking into consideration their specific needs and required functionality.

It is important for everyone to look beyond just design and aesthetics when selecting a door. While those are important aspects, there are numerous other features that contribute to your safety and overall experience. So, choose wisely and consider all the aspects before making a decision.

I am always there to support you in finding the right door.

Love to discuss with you more about the doors.

I can be contacted on

✉ Jitendra@dormak.com

✆ +91 9251441024

Thanks

Chapter 9

KNOW YOUR DOOR FRAME WORK

When Door Jamb (frames) are Installed While Construction Stage:

A) Structure of House

Villa	
Apartment or building	

B) Type of Door Jamb Installed

Stone	
Wood	
Metal	
Width of Rebate	

C) Main Door

Location	Exposed/Covered
Height	
Width	
Design	As per the frame, if it supports that design.
Hardware	As per the frame needs to choose
Fire Rating	As per the frame (Limited Option).
Acoustical Rating	Limited STC possible
Safety Door	Possible only when double rebate frame install.

D) Bed Room

Height	
Width	
Design	As per the frame, if it supports that design.
Hardware	As per the frame needs to choose.
Fire Rating	As per the frame (Limited Option).

E) Toilet Door

Height	
Width	
Design	As per the frame, if it supports that design.
Hardware	As per the frame needs to choose
Wet Area	Need to check the same.
Ventilation	Louvers can be fixed
Light	If natural light required, then glass panel can be fixed

F) Balcony Door

Height	
Width	
Design	As per the frame, if it supports that design.
Hardware	As per the frame needs to choose.
Location	Exposed to sun or not and size of porch outside.
Light	If natural light required, then glass panel can be fixed.

When Door Jamb (Frames) are Not Installed

A) Structure of House

Villa	
Apartment or building	

B) Weather Condition

C) Main Door

Location	Exposed/Covered
Height	If the height is above 8 feet, the door should be designed with a special structure for higher performance.
Width	
Design and Finish	Can choose design as required and plan the frame accordingly
Hardware	Based on hardware, we can choose the door frame and thickness of the door. Need to consider factors such as concealed hinges, concealed door closers, and digital lock if required.
Fire Rating	We can ascertain the required fire rating and choose the appropriate door accordingly.
Acoustical Rating	30-42 dB is possible. Need to choose as per the requirement.
Safety Door Outside	Required/Not Required
Wall Width Cover	Do you want to cover the whole wall width by frame?
Interior of The House	Sometimes, the door is required to be flush with the front wall. And, at that time frames and hardware needs to plan accordingly.
Paneling	Need to plan the frame and finish.

D) Bed Room Door

Height	
Width	
Design and Finish	Can choose design as required and plan the frame accordingly.
Hardware	As per the hardware, we can choose the required door and frame.
Fire Rating	We can ascertain the required fire rating and choose the door.
Acoustical Rating	30-42 dB possible. Need to choose as per the requirement.
Interior Of the House	Sometimes, door is required to be flush with the front wall. And, at that time frames and hardware needs to plan accordingly.

E) Toilet Door

Height	
Width	
Design	Can choose design as required and plan the frame accordingly.
Hardware	As per the hardware we can choose the rest.
Wet Area	Need to check the same.
Ventilation	Louvers can be fixed.
Light	If natural light is required, then glass panel can be fixed.

F) Balcony Door

Height	
Width	
Design	Can choose design as required and plan the frame accordingly.
Hardware	As per the hardware we can choose the rest.
Location	Exposed to sun or not and size of porch outside.

NOTES: ✍

www.ingramcontent.com/pod-product-compliance
Ingram Content Group UK Ltd.
Pitfield, Milton Keynes, MK11 3LW, UK
UKHW041821200726
13854UKWH00001BA/427